NEILL & SUMMERHILL
A Man and His Work
a pictorial study by John Walmsley

Penguin Books

Penguin Books Ltd, Harmondsworth,
Middlesex, England
Penguin Books Inc., 7110 Ambassador Road,
Baltimore, Md 21207, U.S.A.
Penguin Books Australia Ltd, Ringwood,
Victoria, Australia

First published 1969
Photographs copyright © John Walmsley, 1969
Text copyright © Leila Berg and contributors, 1969

Made and printed in Great Britain by
Butler & Tanner Ltd, Frome and London
Set in Lumitype Univers

Contributors

David Barton, ex-Summerhill pupil
Leila Berg
Virginia Charles, ex-Summerhill pupil
Michael Duane, ex-head of Risinghill School
Lucy Francis, ex-Summerhill teacher, now head
of Kingsmuir School
Erna Gal, ex-Summerhill teacher
Gwen Horsfield, parent of a Summerhill pupil
R. F. Mackenzie, ex-head of Braehead School,
now head of Summerhill School, Aberdeen
Bill MacKinnon, ex-Summerhill teacher, now
deputy head of Kilquhanity School
A. L. Morton, ex-Summerhill teacher
Vivian Morton, ex-Summerhill teacher
Willa Muir, ex-Summerhill teacher, worked
with Neill at his first school in Hellerau, Saxony
A. S. Neill
Kirstie Ollendorf, ex-Summerhill cook
Greeba Pilkington, ex-Summerhill matron
Ilse Ollendorf Reich, wife of Wilhelm Reich
Peter Reich, photographer and son of Ilse and
Wilhelm Reich
John Walmsley
Marjorie Watts, ex-probation officer
Summerhill pupils and teachers: Barbara,
Jonathan, Kurt, Mich, Simon (junior),
Simon (senior), Simon (teacher)

The impressions and memories of Neill were
collected by Leila Berg.

My first few days at
Summerhill were spent
adjusting to the school's
atmosphere and in convincing
some of the younger children that
I wasn't going to let them borrow my
cameras; nor was I going to lend them
sixpence each 'only until the morning post
comes'. The children were immediately friendly
and straightforward. If someone objected to being
photographed at a particular moment, or objected for
one reason or another to your presence in their room, they
just said so, and that was that, for no one in Summerhill is
more important than anyone else.

John Walmsley

It's different from other schools. I come from a secondary modern, and it's just like coming out of the dark and into the light.

The whole idea of the thing is different. The lessons are different. Summerhill isn't based on trying to make you *learn*, trying to make you learn your mathematics. . . . It's trying to make you learn about life, a community. You learn from the community, you learn from the meetings, you go through your own little experiences . . . which work out. The whole idea is to be yourself, but not to interfere with other people's ideas and what they're running about and doing. You can be yourself as long as you don't annoy other people. *Simon (senior)*

The 'garden' in front of the school certainly was unkempt, with bits of wood and corrugated iron about — being busily used by several small groups of children, mostly boys, making 'secret camps'. My heart warmed to the unkemptness. I was shown round by a matter-of-fact chatty eleven-year-old. At some point I said something half-inquiringly to the effect that he seemed to be very happy at the school. He was surprised. 'Of course,' he said. 'Everyone is happy here.' *Marjorie Watts*

Very many years ago at Summerhill, Neill
noticed that there was a queue of people
waiting for the lavatory downstairs. It seemed
odd. He went upstairs. Same thing. So a boy
climbed in, and discovered that someone had
locked the doors from the inside and climbed
out again. Neill went to the staffroom and told
them what had happened, and a young Oxford
graduate said happily, 'Yes. It was me. I've
been waiting all my life to do that. And at last I've
found a place where I can.'
Neill commented drily, 'We do tend to
attract them.'   *Leila Berg*

I'd rather be somewhere else than at school. But if I have to be at school, I'd sooner be at Summerhill than anywhere else. Even Summerhill has its bad times. The smaller kids sometimes break out. But they grow out of it. They get used to self-government. They realize what self-government is, and then they become a member of the community. They realize they're not just little kids any more. *Kurt*

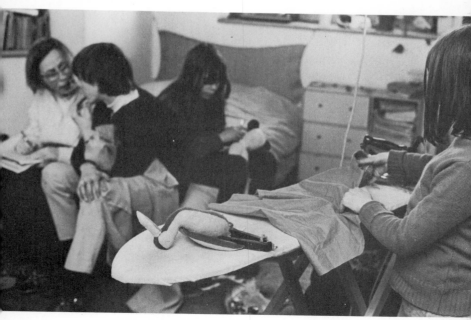

Last term, the older kids had just left, and a few of us were just getting to be the older ones. And it's quite a responsibility.

We got a lot of new kids — about fifteen, I think. And they were so terrible. And they would have been all right if they'd been left alone. But we had a lot of other kids who wanted to influence them, rampaging up and down the corridors, wrecking our rooms. And we went up to Neill in tears. And he said there wasn't much he could do, and we would have to try and cope as best we could. We felt, 'Fuck you, Neill!' We felt some of them should be chucked out — they were too disgusting to cope with.

Then we felt we really could cope if we made an effort. We wanted Neill to chuck them out because it would make our life easier. But then we felt sorry for *them*. So we thought we'd give it a try for another two terms. And in fact they've been a lot better.

Barbara

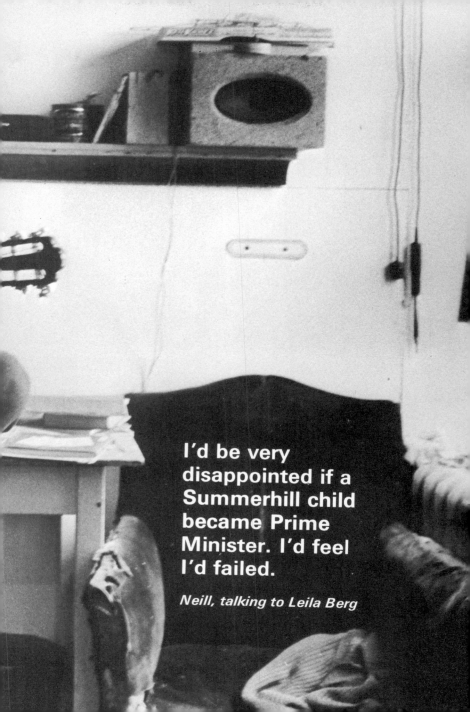

I'd be very disappointed if a Summerhill child became Prime Minister. I'd feel I'd failed.

Neill, talking to Leila Berg

I remember a boy who was got rid of from his public school for dishonesty. He was seventeen, and his father sent him down to Summerhill on a half ticket.

Virginia Charles

I've been here nearly four
years. I came when I was
about nine. I like the way
of the lessons, the
workshop especially. I like
the small classes. When
I first came, for about two
years I never went to any
lessons. I just played. But
now I go to a lot.

Jonathan

When the children first come here, one of the first things they go to is arts or crafts, as being something different from sitting in a classroom. Their path back to lessons, if you like, is through the free approach of the art and craft field where they come in and do pretty well what they like. There are certain restrictions obviously, as to what they do with certain tools, because there are a lot of dangerous tools in the workshop. For instance, only one person goes on the lathe at a time, and nobody else leans against it or starts poking at it. But within those very few restrictions they come and go as they please.

Someone was reading to me a quote from Blackie, the H.M.I. who has written this book about primary education, and he said he thought that junior school kids could use, perhaps, a hammer and a saw; and this would lead up to secondary modern schools, where you could use lathes, brazing torches, that sort of thing. We use all these here. And children from five use a lathe. *Simon (teacher)*

Had Neill chosen, I'm sure he could have made his mark as an actor. There is a thread of economy running through so many activities associated with Neill that has always intrigued me, and this is ever present in his acting and play-writing. Anyone who has received a letter from him will know exactly what I mean. This economy is evident when he tells a story. It is there to a large degree when he dances. Not a word wasted in letter or story. No violent movement, yet in perfect harmony with the rhythm of the dance. *Bill MacKinnon*

A small group of kids had gathered round Neill. I was sitting among them. And the number slowly grew. Neill, as he usually did, built his story round the people present. Thus, I was made the carrier of some very important papers (unspecified) from America to England that some 'enemies' (unspecified) tried to take away from me. The children and staff of Summerhill, especially those present, were assigned important roles in the foiling of all attempts of the villains to steal the papers. If by some chance any of the children present had not been assigned some strategic role, they would interrupt Neill to make sure he would find a place to fit them in. The story ended with all of us victoriously defending the papers and chasing the enemy away. The spell which Neill cast over all of us left an indelible impression. It was so real that on that same evening two little girls whose room was next to mine came up to me, and in a conspiratorial way asked me whether I really had those papers in my room.   *Ilse Ollendorf Reich*

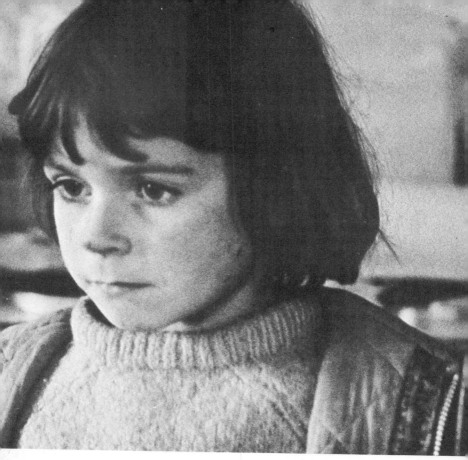

From time to time everybody in the school had nicknames and diminutives. But Neill was very conscientious, and always addressed you by your proper first name. Other staff, if they knew you well, might call you by your nickname. But Neill never risked it — not because he didn't want to be matey, but because he knew nicknames are very often two-edged, and can be given you against your will, something you really hate. He was at once curiously aware and yet unaware of what went on in the school. *David Barton*

Recently I wrote to ask him if
some friends could visit the
school on a certain Monday.
He replied that since they have
forty visitors a week the kids
had made a rule that they
should be allowed only on
Saturday, and if he broke the
rule he would quite likely be
fined his pudding.

Gwen Horsfield

What strikes you immediately, coming from the world outside and talking to the kids at Summerhill, is that you can't tell the boys from the girls. This is important. It's not just hair styles and jeans. The girls are so self-reliant and the boys so concerned, the girls so calmly tough and the boys so gentle. No boy's voice has that conditioned flick of off-handedness that says, 'I am male.' They are interested voices, friendly and lightly generous, and their bodies are not tautly aggressive but trusting. You are startled when you hear their names. You begin to wonder how early children are warped in the world outside, dumped straight from the cradle on to one side of the line they must never step over, separated from one another and from their complete selves, permanently angered. Neill once said, at a progressive school conference, listening to them talk about how to keep the boys from the girls and pressed for his opinion, 'Why don't you put up barbed wire?' *Leila Berg*

The only thing I used to get annoyed about with Neill was that he'd come round and talk to them and say hello, and they'd say, 'Show Neill what we've done in lessons', and he wouldn't look at it. And I'd say, 'Oh, *Neill*! I wish you'd be interested in what they're doing. You seem to think that all children hate lessons! But then he'd tell them a story. They were always about themselves, you know, these stories. He would use them psychologically, but not at all in a heavy way; and they would have the most wonderful adventures. He'd say, 'And then Johnny said, "No, I won't! I won't go up in that aeroplane. It isn't safe. I'm frightened."' And the child would say, 'I never said that! I would go! I . . . I went!' *Lucy Francis*

Neill, you know, could sit
through a whole school meeting
without speaking. I can't. And
many people have said they
can't. Neill does it without any
difficulty whatsoever.

Lucy Francis

I remember he gave a public lecture in Leiston.
And one boy who was a day-boy went. Somebody asked Neill if the children were afraid of
him. And Neill said, 'No. Never.' And then
somebody asked him about swearing, and Neill
said, 'Oh, we just let them swear; and after a
bit they get bored with it, and stop.' And Johnny
put up his hand and said, oh no, that wasn't
true, Neill was wrong there; they didn't stop,
because after a while it had become a habit — he
was stuck in this habit himself. So then I put up
my hand and said, 'It may be true what Johnny
said, that some children never get over swearing,
but Johnny's proved it's true that no child is
afraid of Neill, for Johnny stands up in a public
lecture and contradicts him and Neill takes it.'

Lucy Francis

After Neill had stayed the night with us, I got
the idea of working at Summerhill. I wrote to
him and asked for a job. He replied by telegram,
*Come at once. Help with cooking. Low wages.
Hard work.*

So off I went to Wales, thinking I'd be
helping an experienced cook. But I found the
girl I was to work with was as inexperienced
as myself. And when I told Neill I'd never
cooked for more than five in my life, and there
were over a hundred in the school, he just said,
'Well, lassie, you know how to multiply.'

Kirstie Ollendorf

I met Neill first on a lovely late summer day in
1927, when I went to Summerhill to be
interviewed for a job. I was nervous – a job was
a job in those hard days. Besides, I had read
some of his books and liked the sound of him.
I suppose I expected an interview of the
conventional kind. Of course no such thing
happened. Neill threw me right off my guard
by asking, 'What made you take up teaching?'
I could only say, 'For want of anything better
to do.' At least it was honest. He offered me
the job with little more ado.   *A. L. Morton*

Round about 1949, we heard
there was going to be a
government inspection. At our
weekly staff meeting Neill said,
'I'm going to pass round a bit of
paper, and I want you to put
down any qualifications you've
got, so that I've got something
to wave at them.'

When he got it back, he was
absolutely amazed to find
everyone had recognized
qualifications. ('D'ye mean
you've really got an M.A.?!!')
He hadn't taken any of us on
for that.   *Vivian Morton*

I met him when he was already over eighty.
I think he was wearing jeans. He was tired after
a hard day, and a fatiguing journey. He almost
apologized for travelling first class, pointing out
that it was less tiring that way, and he got more
reading done.   *R. F. Mackenzie*

I remember the parents coming at weekends. And they would say to Neill, 'What can I do, Neill? I don't know what to do.' And Neill would say, 'Well, I've got plenty to do. I don't know what *you* want to get on with.' And they would say, 'I'm bored.' And he'd say, 'Well, everyone is bored before they start doing something.' *Lucy Francis*

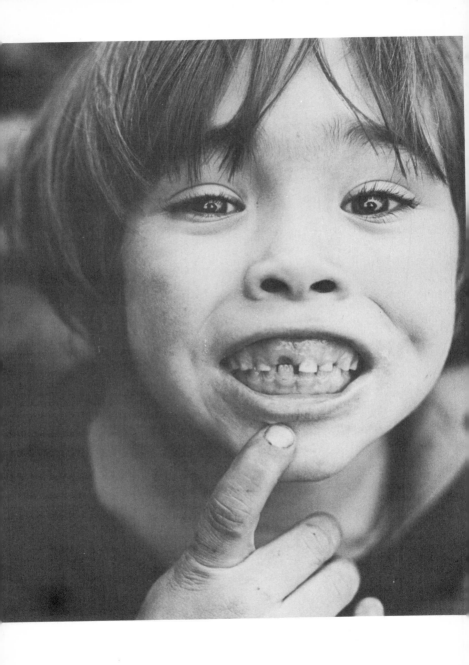

Picasso couldn't get a job teaching art in a state schoo

He's no certificate. *A. S. Neill*

Neill picked me up in Oslo, where I had fled from the Nazis. I was staying with Wilhelm Reich, and Neill came round and we talked about music. A few nights later he phoned and said would I come with him to Summerhill and teach music there. It was April '39. But I was an almost total stranger. On the journey we didn't speak at all. He wanted his peace. I wanted my peace. Outside he is so detached, inside not a bit. He is so witty and sensitive. His whole life is devoted to . . . that children should be free. He doesn't interfere, he doesn't say, he doesn't preach. He lets the children solve their own problems.

Erna Ga.

Oh, he's a fabulous person. First thing you think of when you think of Neill is his sense of humour — which is actually highly warped, but still funny. Then you think of him as being absent-minded as well. Because he can never remember if he's told you which joke or anything. He's a lousy teacher. You think of him as being not so much a member of staff as just being someone who has nothing at all to do with the running of the school, and he's just there to deal with kids. He's almost always on the kids' side, rather than being with the staff. Which is a pretty good deal. *Mich*

I remember him repairing a fence one Sunday morning when one of the local church dignitaries went by on his way to morning service. He asked Neill why he was doing such work on a Sunday. Neill replied, 'Where is your wife?'

'She's at home, making the dinner' was the answer, at which Neill turned away.

Gwen Horsfield

I sat listening to the Council meeting. Neill, with a small child curled up on his lap, looked more like a shepherd relaxing after a day on the hills than a headmaster.   *Michael Duane*

He is so many things to me. I don't see him as a teacher, an educationalist, a man of letters or books. I always see him in my mind *outside* . . . shirtless, doing something with his hands, putting bricks on a wall or something — not a headmaster, totally unlike a headmaster.   *Virginia Charles*

Not so very long ago he said to me, 'The only thing I regret in my life is that I didn't sin more when I was young.'   *Willa Muir*

Got better food than any other school I've been to — and I've been to four or five. Other schools you get about a spoonful of macaroni cheese. Here you get roast beef, roast potatoes, pork, treacle tart, jam tart, greengages . . . just about everything.

Also I like C Night (Cinema) when we have crisps. You're allowed to tear up loads of paper and use it for confetti — as long as you sweep it up again. And that's fun.

There are loads of people who are nice. But there are those people who are horrible.

I like it because we have a lab for science. In my old school we didn't even have a lab. We just had to write about how fish breathe. It has more equipment than any other school I've been to. The lab, the workshop. . . . In my old school we were never allowed to *use* things like that.

Simon (junior)

He was always painting things. Once he painted the garage doors bright blue, and painted an enormous monster on it like a praying mantis. We used to run past it with our eyes shut. Later I used to think it was odd that a psychiatrist should do this. But he knew fear was important. He used to tell us terrifying stories because he knew we loved them. *Virginia Charles*

People often ask how Summerhill
children are able to adapt to the hard
outside world after their rather
exceptional education. The fact is, they
adapt, on the average, considerably
better than most, and I believe the
reason is that they have lived for years
in a small but really functioning
society, all members of which they
really come to see as having rights
and interests that demand equal
respect to their own. Of course there
is a complex criss-cross of conflicts,
loves, hates, feuds and alliances.
Without these there would be no life.
But there is no deep, permanent gulf
cutting off any group from another.

A. L. Morton

There was once a little shop near the school, a tuckshop, and the chap who used to run it used to cheat the kids all the time out of their pennies and halfpennies. So Sandy, a mad kid but very clever, decided he'd put a stop to it. So he went into the shop — it had a bell that rang whenever anyone came in — and then went out again, quickly. And Sandy kept doing this, over and over again. So eventually the shopkeeper took down the bell — which was what Sandy wanted. So then the kids formed a long line, and they passed out everything that was in the shop. . . . *Greeba Pilkington*

Oh, villainous Tommy. He was another extraordinary boy, very intelligent. They had a larder with an iron grating in front to stop people pinching things. But the milk kept disappearing from the bottles. So eventually two people kept watch at night. And Tommy turned up, with masses of pipes and tubes, and started siphoning the milk out through the grating. He had an affinity for reptiles. He used to take lizards to the cinema. *Virginia Charles*

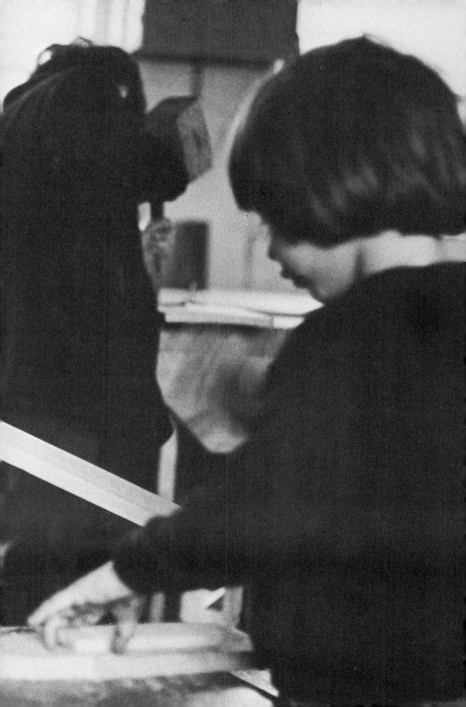

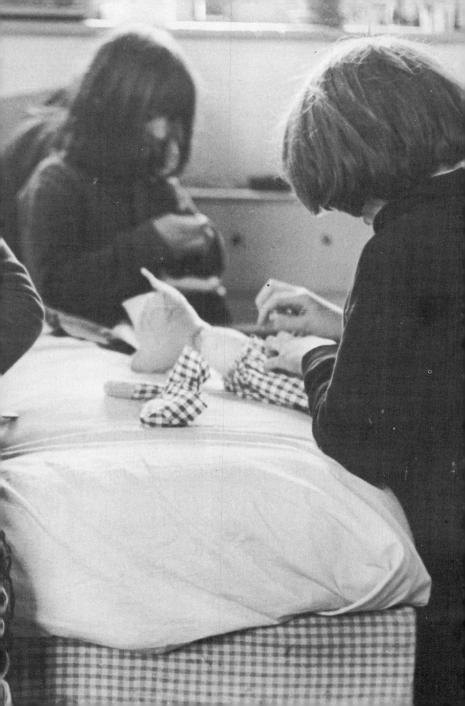

He gave me away at my wedding. He was terrified of going into church. He was practically wetting himself in the car, and kept saying, 'What do I do? What do I do?' And I had to keep reassuring him. He was trembling. And of course he was a great success and made a magnificent speech. We'd done it in a place that does everything — reception rooms, changing rooms. . . . He'd hired a suit that didn't fit. And he sat on the edge of the bed with a huge piece of brown paper for wrapping up his clothes, saying over and over again, 'Where's my string? I canna find my string!' It was amazing how afraid he was. He felt it was hypocrisy and something dreadful would happen to him. Yet I know he was so pleased to be there with me. *Virginia Charles*

When he was in New York in December 1968, Neill called me up one day and said, 'Let's go for a walk, lad, I can't stand being cooped up in the city.' I was living on Staten Island at the time, and drove in to pick him up. We took the ferry back to Staten Island for lunch and a walk on the beach. Neill was sitting with his back to the Statue of Liberty, and as we passed close to it I said, 'Neill, look! There's the Statue of Liberty!'

'Oh my,' he said in a startled voice, 'I haven't seen her in a long time.' And passengers on the Staten Island Ferry were startled to see an elderly gentleman stand up, turn around, and with the deference of a schoolboy to a lady, doff his hat and bow. *Peter Reich*

Adam and Eve: the first love-in

There was the day when there was a charabanc load of visitors. The kids hated it, the charabanc load coming up to look at them. The dining table was laid out with a beautiful afternoon tea, everything on it. We had a big bell that was used at an emergency to summon people for a special meeting in the hall. Tony rang it. The visitors all trooped into the hall. They were very pleased and excited — a special meeting! And while they were out of the room the kids cleared everything off the table.   *Greeba Pilkington*

A new
six-year-old,
writing home:
'There is a
nice chap here
called Neill.

I like him.'

Lucy Francis